THE HUMAN MACHINE

Human

Emotions

LINDA BOZZO

Rourke
Educational Media

rourkeeducationalmedia.com

Before Reading:

Building Academic Vocabulary and Background Knowledge

Before reading a book, it is important to tap into what your child or students already know about the topic. This will help them develop their vocabulary, increase their reading comprehension, and make connections across the curriculum.

1. *Look at the cover of the book. What will this book be about?*
2. *What do you already know about the topic?*
3. *Let's study the Table of Contents. What will you learn about in the book's chapters?*
4. *What would you like to learn about this topic? Do you think you might learn about it from this book? Why or why not?*
5. *Use a reading journal to write about your knowledge of this topic. Record what you already know about the topic and what you hope to learn about the topic.*
6. *Read the book.*
7. *In your reading journal, record what you learned about the topic and your response to the book.*
8. *After reading the book complete the activities below.*

Content Area Vocabulary

Read the list. What do these words mean?

addiction
contempt
cultures
depression
digestion
expressions
imbalance
motivation
psychologist
universal

After Reading:

Comprehension and Extension Activity

After reading the book, work on the following questions with your child or students in order to check their level of reading comprehension and content mastery.

1. *How does dopamine give us a sense of reward? (Summarize)*
2. *Why do people from different cultures share universal emotions? (Infer)*
3. *Which system is thought to be the center for emotions? (Asking Questions)*
4. *Which emotion do you feel when you eat your favorite food? (Text to Self Connection)*
5. *How can you read someone's emotions? (Asking Questions)*

Extension Activity

We often only think of common emotions like happy, sad, and mad. But there are many other words used to express emotions. Build a vocabulary of words for naming emotions by partnering with a friend and see how many emotion words you can write down in one minute. Use these words in your writing and when discussing your feelings.

TABLE OF CONTENTS

LIFE WITH EMOTIONS

Chances are you've experienced happiness, love, or anger. This means you've experienced emotions! Emotions are powerful feelings. They can change suddenly and we don't always understand them. One day you wake up feeling joyful. Another day you wake up feeling gloomy. You might not even know where your emotions come from or why they are present.

We know emotions can be influenced by things like the amount of sleep we get or stress. Sometimes it's not easy to deal with our emotions, but it's hard to imagine what our lives would be like without them.

Getting the right of amount of rest and sleep plays an important role in how we feel.

Robert Plutchik (1927 - 2006) was a **psychologist** who created the wheel of emotions. He said there are eight primary emotions: anger, fear, sadness, disgust, surprise, anticipation, trust, and joy. Each of these has a place on the wheel. Like colors, he said emotions can have different intensities. Also like colors, a primary emotion can mix with another primary emotion to form another emotion.

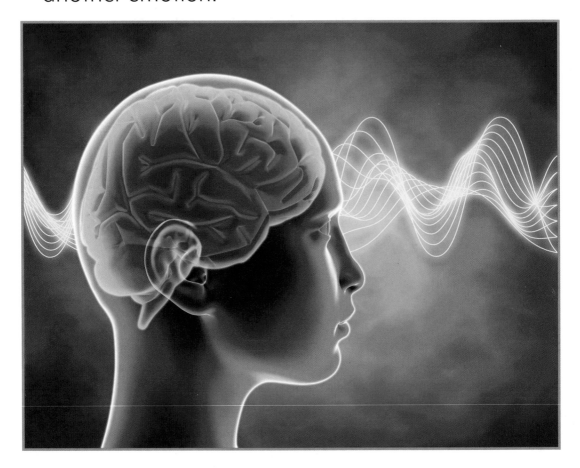

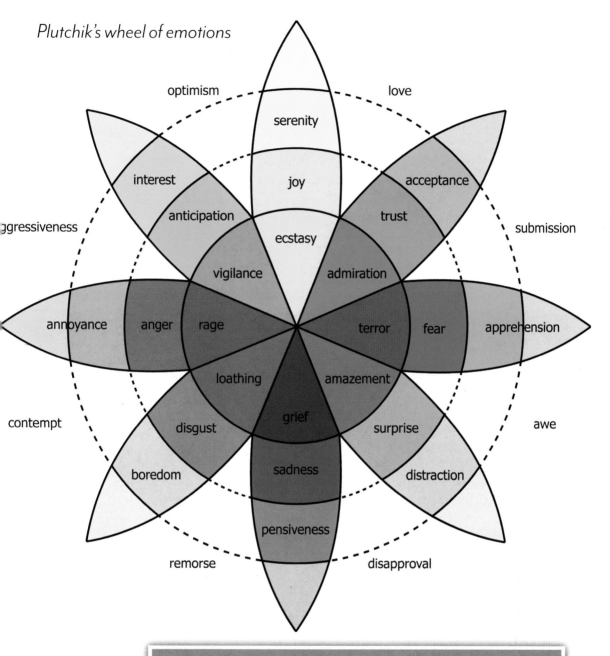

Plutchik's wheel of emotions

In a recent study, researchers were able to identify 27 distinct categories of emotion and how they blend together in our everyday lives.

SENDING SIGNALS

Think your emotions come from your heart? Think again! The average human brain has an estimated 100 billion nerve cells called neurons. These neurons communicate through electrical and chemical signals. Chemical messengers, called neurotransmitters, send signals from one neuron to the next.

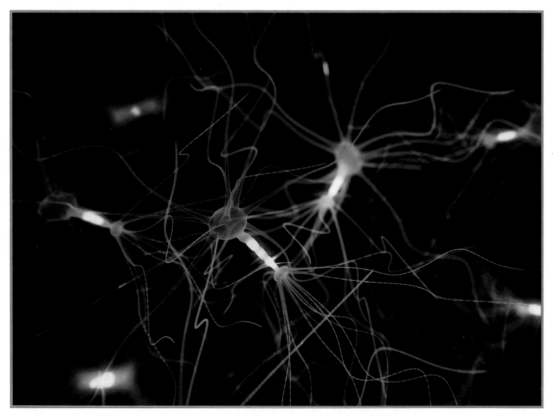

Networks of neurons interact together to process information in the brain.

Serotonin is a neurotransmitter. Some researchers think it is involved in mood balance as well as sleep, appetite and **digestion**, memory, sexual function, and social behavior. But what happens if the brain doesn't make enough serotonin? Some say it causes a chemical **imbalance** that can lead to **depression**.

If for more than two weeks you have feelings of sadness, loneliness, or a loss of interest in things you once enjoyed, you may be experiencing depression. Being unable to study, eat, or sleep properly are other common signs that you should seek professional help from a doctor.

KNOW THE WARNING SIGNS OF SUICIDE

- Talking about wanting to die or threatening to kill themselves
- Searching for ways to kill themselves, like searching online or buying a weapon like a gun
- Talking about, writing, or posting on social media about feeling hopeless or having no reason to live
- Talking about feeling trapped or in unbearable pain
- Talking about being a burden to others
- Increasing the use of alcohol or drugs
- Acting anxious or agitated; behaving recklessly
- Sleeping too little or too much
- Withdrawing or isolating themselves
- Showing rage or talking about seeking revenge
- Showing extreme mood swings

If you suspect that you or someone you know is suicidal, take immediate action by seeking help from a trusted adult. For 24-hour suicide prevention and support in the U.S., call the National Suicide Prevention Lifeline at 1-800-273-TALK or text 741741 to text with a trained Crisis Counselor.

Another neurotransmitter that relates to emotion is dopamine. The major dopamine pathways in the brain help control movement, **motivation**, and reward.

Dopamine receptors in the brain tell us that what we just experienced is worth getting more of. It gives us a sense of reward. As a result, our desire to experience that feeling again increases. Let's face it, things that are rewarding tend to make us feel good. We want more! Not enough dopamine? You can lose pleasure in normal day-to-day activities. The things we once enjoyed no longer bring us the same feeling.

Drugs such as cocaine, nicotine, and heroin cause a huge rise in dopamine. This results in a "high" that people feel causing them to seek out those drugs again and again. It's this brain reward that can lead to drug abuse and **addiction**.

Some people get a dopamine rush from a thrilling ride on a roller coaster.

Low dopamine levels in the body may be a result of poor nutrition, lack of sleep, and use of street drugs, just to name a few. Some common symptoms include: always being bored, not feeling satisfied, tiredness, decrease in physical activity, and no desire for exercise.

Eating healthy, exercising daily, and taking medications are several treatments used with hopes of increasing serotonin and dopamine in the brain.

There's no way to measure serotonin or dopamine levels in the brain. This makes it difficult for people in the medical field to agree on whether or not chemical imbalances actually occur in the brain.

EMOTIONAL CENTER

The limbic system, a group of structures in the brain, is most often thought to be the main center for our emotions. Feel angry? Scared? Your limbic system is probably in action.

The taste of homemade chicken soup can provide comfort on a stressful day.

The limbic system gathers information from the environment through our senses. This can produce emotions. Maybe you smell something that gives you comfort because it makes you remember something pleasant. Hearing a song or seeing a particular object might remind you of a special moment in your life.

The limbic system is thought by some to include the amygdala and the hippocampus. These structures are closely connected with emotion, memory, and learning. We know that there are many structures in the brain connected to our emotions. However, scientists do not agree on which ones are part of the limbic system.

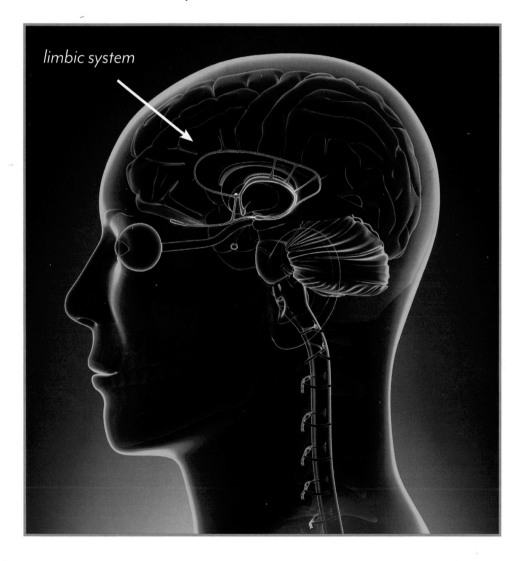

limbic system

The amygdala is thought to play a part in processing emotions such as pleasure, anger, and fear. It's best known for where we learn to fear something. For example, if you've ever been bitten by a dog, it's your amygdala that stores that event, which can result in you fearing dogs.

The hippocampus takes current events and our emotional reactions to them and stores them as long-term memories. Researchers say that memories which happen during an emotional state are more easily remembered somewhere down the road.

Let's say you've had a heated argument with someone. You become very angry. Many years later you see that person again. You're more likely to remember the argument thanks to your hippocampus!

Researchers say negative events are remembered more accurately than positive or neutral events because of the emotion involved.

When it comes to emotion, the hypothalamus is another structure often considered part of the limbic system. It causes an unconscious response called "fight or flight." When it senses possible danger, it automatically puts our body into survival mode. It tells us to fight danger or run from it.

The limbic system also plays an important part in our body's everyday functions such as hunger, breathing, and the beating of our heart. And while scientists continue to debate which structures are part of the limbic system, one thing we know for sure is that we can't live without it.

The Limbic System

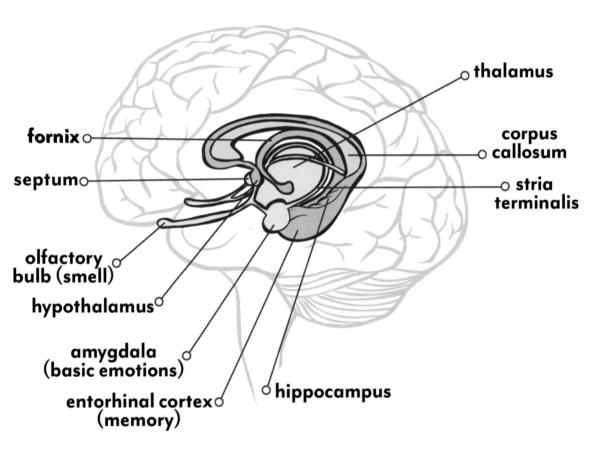

This cross-section of a human brain shows the limbic system and related structures.

EMOTIONS IN MOTION

Everyone experiences good and bad emotions. They can come and go quickly. They can last for days. No matter the emotion, it's important to recognize, feel, and show them in a healthy and safe way.

Sometimes we feel joy. Other times we feel sadness. We can even feel joy and sadness in the same day. Emotions can range from mild to strong.

Psychologists often refer to joy as an emotional state created by positive thoughts and feelings. Perhaps eating your favorite food brings you feelings of joy and a smile to your face. But you can't be happy all the time.

While we might try to avoid sadness, it's a normal part of life. Sadness is an emotion that everyone feels at times. It can be connected with pain or loss. Most people have felt sadness over losing a loved one or a friend. As long as it doesn't happen too often or last for a long period of time, it's okay to feel sad.

EMOTIONS EXPRESSED

Facial and body movements have long been known as a way to read emotions. If your friend's eyes are wide and her eyebrows raised, she may be surprised. If your teacher's fists are clenched and his body is tense, he may be angry.

Charles Darwin was the first to suggest that human **expressions**, especially of the face, were innate and not learned by an individual. In his book *The Expression of the Emotions in Man and Animals*, published in 1872, Darwin shared his theory that body expressions that occur during basic emotions are **universal**.

Researchers from around the world and different **cultures** have found strong evidence for the universal facial expressions of seven emotions: anger, **contempt**, disgust, fear, joy, sadness, and surprise. For instance, people in the United States make the same face for sadness as people on the other side of the world.

Studies confirm that the same expressions were found in people who were born blind, without having the opportunity to copy the muscle movements from others.

Other studies show that emotions and how we express them are learned in part through experience and influenced by our social environment. For example, a child who lives in an unfriendly social environment may develop an emotional response of fear or anxiety.

HOPE FOR THE FUTURE

Our emotions are an important part of being human. Every day we experience new situations and challenges that we respond to using our emotions.

As research continues, new discoveries are made about the complicated network of body structures that create emotions. This research can help treat people with emotional issues. It also can help us further understand ourselves and the way we respond to the world around us.

GLOSSARY

addiction (uh-DIK-shun): uncontrollable use of habit-forming drugs

contempt (kuhn-TEMPT): total lack of respect

cultures (KUHL-churs): the cultures of groups of people are their ways of life, ideas, customs, and traditions

depression (di-PRESH-uhn): sadness or gloominess

digestion (duh-JESS-chuhn): the process of breaking down food in the stomach and other organs so that it can be absorbed into the blood

expressions (ek-SPRESH-uhns): the looks on people's faces

imbalance (im-BAL-ens): a lack of balance

motivation (MOH-tuh-va-shun): the condition of being eager to work or act

psychologist (sye-KOL-uh-jist): someone who studies people's minds and emotions and the ways that people behave

universal (yoo-nuh-VUR-suhl): something that is found everywhere

INDEX

SHOW WHAT YOU KNOW

1. What is the limbic system?

2. What are some common warning signs of depression?

3. What is one way the limbic system gathers information from the environment?

4. Which emotions are considered to be universal emotions?

5. What are some ways we express emotions?

FURTHER READING

Ford, Jean, *Coping with Moods*, Mason Crest Publishers, 2014.

Frances, Suzanne, *Inside Out: The Junior Novelization*, Random House, 2015.

Petelinsek, Kathleen, *Feelings and Emotions*, The Child's World, 2015.

ABOUT THE AUTHOR

Linda Bozzo is an award-winning author of more than 60 nonfiction books for children. She enjoys writing about science and has always been fascinated by the wonders of the human body. She lives in New Jersey with her family where she shares her books by visiting schools. To learn more about Linda you can visit her website: lindabozzo.com.

Meet The Author!
www.meetREMauthors.com

www.rourkeeducationalmedia.com

PHOTO CREDITS: Cover, Title Pg & Pg 3 ©pixelliebe, Pgs 3 - 32 (top bar) ©AniphaeS, Pg 4 ©digitalskillet, Pg 5 ©Juanmonino, Pg 6 ©undefined undefined, Pg 7 ©Machine Elf 1735, Pg 8 ©Polina Shuvaeva, Pg 9 ©FatCamera, Pg 11 ©lzf, Pg 12 ©By Best_photo_studio, Pg 13 ©By Nic Vilceanu, Pg 14 ©By Ben Gingell, Pg 15 ©monkeybusinessimages, Pg 16 ©rez-art, Pg 17 ©By decade3d - anatomy online, Pg 18 ©By fotosparrow, Pg 19 ©KatarzynaBialasiewicz, Pg 20 ©Dean Mitchell, Pg 21 ©mediaphotos, Pg 22 ©eli_asenova, Pg 23 ©By corbac40, Pg 24 ©ArtMarie, Pg 25 ©kali9, Pg 26 ©SIphotography, Pg 27 ©Riccardo Lennart Niels Mayer, Pg 28 ©Wavebreakmedia, Pg 29 ©phototechno

Edited by: Keli Sipperley
Cover design by: Rhea Magaro-Wallace
Interior design by: Kathy Walsh

Library of Congress PCN Data

Human Emotions / Linda Bozzo
(The Human Machine)
ISBN 978-1-64156-437-3 (hard cover)
ISBN 978-1-64156-563-9 (soft cover)
ISBN 978-1-64156-683-4 (e-Book)
Library of Congress Control Number: 2018930466

Rourke Educational Media
Printed in the United States of America,
North Mankato, Minnesota